JAPANESE LIVING

First published in the United Kingdom in 2007 by Scriptum Editions
an imprint of Co & Bear Productions (UK) Ltd
Copyright © 2007 Co & Bear Productions (UK) Ltd
Photographs copyright © 2007 Noboru Murata

ISBN–10 1 902 686 60 8
ISBN–13 978 1 902 686 60 8

Publisher Beatrice Vincenzini & Francesco Venturi
Executive Director David Shannon
Design Brian Rust

First edition
1 3 5 7 9 10 8 6 4 2

Printed in Italy

JAPANESE LIVING

PHOTOGRAPHY BY NOBORU MURATA

SCRIPTUM EDITIONS

The ancient Taoist scholar Laotse espoused that the true beauty of a room lay in the vacant space enclosed by the roof and walls, rather than the roof and walls themselves. He aspired to an aesthetic ideal of emptiness. True beauty could only be realised in the material world, he held, when it was stripped almost bare, with only the merest suggestion of colour, pattern or texture. The mind, the imagination of the beholder, should be allowed to complete the picture in the mood of the moment.

This is the essence of the Japanese house. Laotse's philosophy was imported to Japan via Zen Buddhism, and went on to become an integral aspect of the Japanese approach to living. The Japanese house thus shuns the decorative, the obvious, the extravagantly showy, in favour of restraint, of emptiness, or what contemporary architects and designers would refer to as minimalism.

When entering a Japanese house for the first time, it is emptiness that first strikes the foreign eye. No art works on the wall, no thick carpets, no bold wallpapers or chandeliers or heavy curtains. The house appears to have been pared back to its essential elements. It seems to be purely functional.

The second thing that becomes apparent is its impermanent state. Interior walls slide open to double the size of a room. At night, futons are pulled from sliding cupboards, built flush with the wall, and put away again in the morning to clear floor space for other uses. From season to season, this mutability becomes even more obvious. In summer, external walls are slid open to bring a sense of the garden beyond inside, as well as cooling breezes. Sliding wooden *shoji* are replaced with ones of bamboo or reed in summer, to improve ventilation. And from summer to autumn to winter to spring, small decorative details mark the passing of the seasons: the scroll in the living-room alcove is changed, or a new flower arrangement appears in the entrance, bearing a blossom or sprig evocative of the time of year.

However, any real understanding of the Japanese house must begin with an appreciation of the materials used in its building. Just as brick and plaster gave European towns their particular appearance, so have wood, bamboo, straw and paper lent Japanese towns and villages their unique look and a powerful sense of continuity that is still evident today.

ALTHOUGH A SAMURAI house, it was built, in 1657, in the farmhouse style, with a hipped and gabled thatch roof. The commoners' entrance is immediately recognisable by its earthen floor, while the neighbouring entrance for aristocrats and samurai is accessed by wooden steps.

A COURTYARD GARDEN, restored using
traditional materials such as white gravel,
cedar moss and raked sand, to create a
meditative garden with the rhythmic
motion of the waves as its theme.

DESPITE THE replacement of the old thatched roof with a replica one in tin, the *Minka*, or farmhouse retains its character. The *mon*, or gate, leading to the garden indicates that the farming family who once lived here were quite prosperous.

THE *ENGAWA*, or veranda, which provides an intermediate space between the interior and the garden – once wrapped around the entire house but now only one section remains. Farmhouses like this were designed for summer living, and the sliding doors of the *engawa* encouraged maximum airflow.

CANDLES AND candlelit lanterns recreate the ambience of old Japan on a timber deck, which provides a tranquil place to enjoy an early-evening cup of tea.

AUTHENTIC DETAILS add character to this building; the earth-floored entrance with its aged wooden doors and an old woven basket bearing a sprig from the garden.

THE GARDEN is a crucial element of the tea house. A simple stone path leads from an outdoor waiting pavilion to a number of different tearooms; the roji, or garden path, symbolises the transition from the mundane world to the spiritually enlightened world of the tea ceremony. A stone wrapped in black cord traditionally acts as a stop sign, signalling that access is prohibitied.

A PAVED STONE path leads the visitor from the informal entrance gate to the main part of the tea school. The gate is called *Amigasamon* because the roof resembles an *amigasa*, a large rain hat made of woven bamboo (*Mon* means 'gate' in Japanese). More than just a directional pointer, the path is an important element in the design of any teahouse.

INSPIRED BY the rural origins of the house, all the
garden plants were sourced from the mountains in
the Chiba prefecture. The overall effect, with the
meandering gravel paths, bound bamboo fencing
and informal plantings, is one of great charm and
rustic simplicity.

23

HANDMADE OILED-PAPER umbrellas, a speciality of Kyoto, sit ready at the entrance for those who venture out from this mountain retreat into the falling snow. These large rain umbrellas are called *bangasa* and the best-quality ones are made to last for years.

EVEN UNDER the weight of deep winter snows, there is no mistaking the elegant entrance to this retreat, with its circular window, freshly swept stone-paved path and porch, and the gentle glimmer of light from inside the *genkan*, or foyer.

THE APPROACH to this villa is through an enormous *tori* gate, a structure that typically marks the entrance to a shrine precinct. From here, a steep driveway sweeps up to the two-storey villa, which was constructed from cypress according to ancient tenets – not a single nail was used. Each roof tile bears the Imperial symbol of the sixteen-petalled chrysanthemum.

THIS QUINTESSENTIAL scene demonstrates the mutability of indoor and outdoor space. The sliding *shoji* walls of the interior room open on to the *engawa*, an intermediate space with glass doors opening on to the veranda and garden beyond.

THE CENTRAL courtyard is referred to by the architect as an 'outer room' because it is designed as an extension of the interior living space – an essential part of the home. Even during winter, this 'outer room' acts as a sun trap.

FLEXIBLE WALLS of woven reed, allow the side passageway to be converted into any number of guises, and to control the light at any time of day. In this respect it resembles the traditional *engawa*, or veranda, with its sliding screens. A modern reinterpretation of the *shoji*, the massive glass doors can be slid back noiselessly on their floor tracks, to be fully concealed within a deep cavity.

SECLUDED IN a leafy garden, high above the historic town of Kamakura, sit two farmhouses transported from the mountainous interior of Japan and reconstructed them here, an unusual sight. The houses were rescued by the owners just days before the village where they stood was to be flooded for a dam project.

THE EARLIEST of the two houses, which dates from 1734, is entered through a traditional *mon*, or gate. Across the garden is the second house, which dates from the late 1700s. Although the original thatched roofs have been replaced, the traditional steep pitch of the roofline remains.

HEAVY SNOW silhouettes the distinctive lines of the traditional thatched *minka,* or people's house. Like its neighbours in this tiny, remote mountain village, it is thatched from grass that grows in the same valley. The ornamented ridge that runs the length of the roof is typical of *minka* architecture. The roof is so steep, with such deep eaves, that walls are barely visible.

THE THICK thatch of the *minka* is bound to a framework of *susudake* bamboo, which has turned black after years of smoke rising from the open hearth at floor level below. (Open hearths in these old country houses have now been largely replaced by stoves with chimneys). The gable end of the roof ridge is adorned with the Shindo family crest, and incorporates a vent for expelling smoke from the hearth.

THIS TYPICAL Kyoto *machiya*, or city house, was built in 1899 and has been lovingly restored by the president of the Kyoto Machiya Preservation Committee. Despite a narrow façade at street level, the house runs back to occupy a substantial site, with beautifully landscaped garden and three whitewashed *kura*, or storehouses.

46

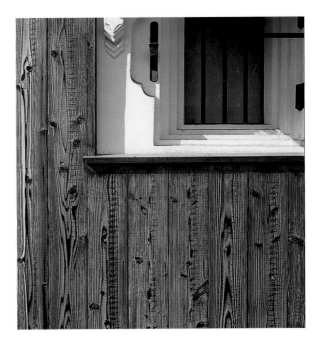

THE *KURA*, or storehouse, of the *machiya* is built with cedar cladding at ground level and white mortar covering the upper level. Deep-set windows, called *takamado*, are just big enough to provide ventilation. Their design is unique to the *kura*.

IN THE STYLE of a Frank Lloyd Wright
house, Kamui was built from textured
brick, to harmonise with the natural
environment. An early nineteenth-
century stone statue from Korea stands
at the approach to the front of the house.

A SIMPLE HOUSE built from natural materials to serve as her weekend retreat and a spiritual sanctuary. A wooden post bears the name of the house, Kamui – from the Japanese characters for 'flower', 'mist' and 'living'.

THE INTERIOR mood of refined rusticity
begins in the garden, the entrance to
which is marked by a finely crafted
bamboo fence and gate

THE SLATTED wooden façade and overhanging tiled eaves are typical of the *machiya*, in this part of old Kyoto. Only the lamp bearing the characters for 'Kinmata' mark it as a *ryokan*, or inn. The paved area outside is washed clean each morning with water from a bamboo bucket.

ARCHITECTURAL ELEGANCE is revealed in the exterior details. The design of the *engawa*, or veranda, railings allows the sunlight to create pleasing shadows throughout the day. The timber facing of an upstairs *demado*, or bay window, gives yet another opportunity for the aesthetic interplay of horizontal and vertical lines.

A LONG CORRIDOR runs from the entrance to the very end of the building. It is broken halfway along its course by a miniature courtyard garden – called a *tsubo* – which allows daylight to enter the ground floor and provides a leafy outlook for the second-storey rooms.

THIS VIEW from the rear garden enables a full appreciation of the structure. The raised floor, referred to as *yuka*, stems back to the architectural style that evolved in Japan in the Yayoi period (300 BC – AD 300) to deal with monsoon conditions. Before the Meiji Restoration of 1868, second storeys were only permitted for aristocratic houses or inns.

THE SMOKE-BLACKENED timbers and the stark white walls and *shoji* screens of the old house create a dramatic backdrop for Hiroyuki Shindo's acclaimed indigo art. To the left of the alcove, a *shoin* window with carved transom – once the preserve of the samurai class – hints at the history of the house, built for a village chief who also collected taxes for the local warlord.

A DISTINCTIVE FEATURE of many houses are the lounge and dining areas occupying a single vast space underneath huge, rough-hewn ceiling beams that span the entire width of each structure. The pine wood throughout the houses has been blackened by centuries of wood smoke from the open hearths, which were common in country.

THE CENTREPIECE of this room is a dining table made especially for the house from Japanese oak. The centre panel pulls out to reveal a stove with three built-in gas rings, on which food can be cooked directly at the table.

THIS MODERN house reveals its debt to ancient Japanese building principles in the internal structure of pillars and beams, which echoes that of temple and shrine architecture. All the internal timber is Canadian cedar.

TRADITIONAL JAPANESE homes have a natural airy, open-plan feel, due in large part to the clever use of intermediate indoor-outdoor spaces. Narrow hallways lead to *engawa*, or verandas, providing a link to the gardens, and staircases climb through open mezzanine levels before continuing upwards to the bedrooms and bathrooms.

ONCE INSIDE the front door, the merchant's shop can be entered directly, while a path leads to the main part of the house. A water well with overhead pulley was typically located here. Beyond the *noren* curtain marking the entrance to the house, a path opens out into the *toriniwa*, or corridor, with its full-height ceilings.

ROOMS ON the upper level open on to a veranda overlooking the garden and with views to the Kyoto hills. The design of the veranda railing is an amalgam of Art Deco and Japanese elements. Wooden *geta, sandals* sit ready in the *genkan*, or foyer, for those venturing out to the garden.

THE MAIN entrance to the genkan is marked by a pair of beautifully panelled *shoji* sliding doors. Their patterning is derived directly from Art Deco motifs, and they divide the terracotta-paved *genkan* from the interior with its luxurious parquet floor of oak and cherry.

STAINED-GLASS WINDOWS in the Art Deco style were commissioned especially. The motif in the long rectangular window, which is repeated around the perimeter of the circular window, is abstracted from the Japanese characters for 'Fushiminomiya', the prince for whom the villa was built. More traditional decorative details are echoed in the panelled ceiling, carved transom, and the play of vertical and horizontal lines evident in the *shoji* paper screen and outer wooden door.

AN INTIMATE tea-ceremony room with tatami floors
leads off from the open-plan living area. Even in
this quiet, more traditional space, bold vertical
windows help to unify the tea room with the rest
of the house. The scroll depicts Daruma, the
ancient Buddhist scholar.

A COLLECTION OF antique, vermilion-red lacquerware, which dates from between the fourteenth and sixteenthth centuries.
The square plate was made around 1900 in the Oribe style by the celebrated potter Rozanjin Kitaoji. The setting, above, called *yotsu-wan*, was traditionally used for food served to priests. The lids of both bowls are designed to be removed and upturned for use as plates.

A BALCONY WRAPS around the living area. In fine weather, massive glass doors can be slid smoothly back on concealed tracks to rest, invisibly, in a deep recess in the supporting pillar. This feature plays on the traditional sliding *shoji* door. This enables the residents to feel as though they are nestled among the forests of Hakone.

THIS FRONT ROOM is reserved for tea ceremony. Here it is set with a brazier and antique silk screen. The lamp-lit *shoin* window, intended as a kind of writing desk, is a typical feature of a samurai home. A built-in hearth also serves as a site where tea masters John McGee and Alexandre Avdulov conduct tea ceremony. The sixteenth-century iron kettle is one of their many beautiful tea utensils.

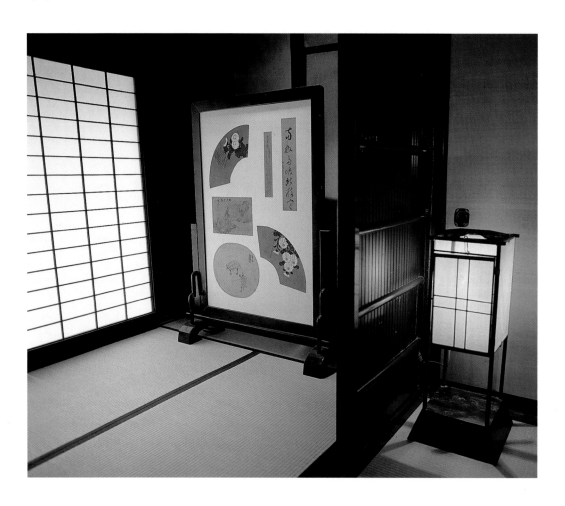

COMPLETELY RESTORED, with new floors laid and the walls replastered,.this house now offers a unique look at living style in the mid-seventeenth century, albeit with a few concessions to modern-day comfort, such as electricity and plumbing. In most other ways it remains true to the original design and ambience.

LOOKING OUT over the garden, the main living room is flooded with natural light, enhancing the warm tones of the tatami floor. In summer the sliding doors slide across to give direct access to the leafy garden, while in winter a set of *shoji* screens can be added to provide insulation from the cold.

94

PURITY AND CLEANLINESS are crucial components
of any tea ceremony, and all the utensils must be
carefully cleaned and prepared before use. This takes
place in the *midsuya*, or anteroom, which is screened
from the view of the guest.

IN FINE WEATHER, the reed blinds along the passageway can be raised to create an additional living area for sunbathing or lounging. Woven reed blinds also hang the full frontage of the internal living area, and can be adjusted to any length.

WOVEN REED has been used for centuries in Japanese homes. When fashioned into blinds and sliding doors, it is perfectly suited to Japan's humid summers, allowing air to circulate while screening out insects and the fiercest of the sun's rays.

THE MOST DISTINCTIVE features of these guest rooms are the delightful hand-painted papers that cover the sliding screens, called *fusuma*, and the decoratively carved transoms above, which gently filter the light.

IN CONTRAST to the vibrant *fusuma* screens,
with their evocations of the natural world,
the rest of the decor is left intentionally
bare, so as not to distract from the scenes
of nature outside. Guests sit on slim
cushions, called *zabuton*, and enjoy a
restorative tea while admiring the view.

HERE A CUP of *hoji-cha* tea sits beside an antique smoking kit – in times past proffered as the traditional welcome to any guest – while a sweet rice cake is served alongside a cup of *matcha*, the powdered whisked green tea served at tea ceremonies.

THE *GENKAN*, or foyers, present a picture of spare and restrained elegance. Details such as the ribbing on the wooden *amado* shutters, and the subtle, beautifully coloured paper-covered doors beyond, point to an interior of great refinement.

GRADUATED, INDIGO-DYED linen screens hang at the entrance to this veranda, gently screening the strong afternoon sun that floods the house and helping to protect the tatami floor mats.

THE APPROACH from the front gate creates an immediate atmosphere of restraint and tranquillity and from the outset binds the house and garden into a unified whole. The tea room can be entered directly from the garden through the *nijiru-guchi*, an opening just large enough to crawl through. The device dates back to samurai times and compelled warriors to remove their swords and humble themselves before entering the tea room.

GUESTS AND CLIENTS are received in the main
reception room. On close inspection this plain
tatami room reveals a wealth of detail, such as
the lacquerware table and lacquer bowls, all
made by Nakamura Sotetsu. Although plain in
appearance, such pieces are works of art, used
for special occasions. They are fashioned in
solid wood and finished with glossy lacquer.

THE ARTIST'S STUDIO is a small, light-filled space, which can be screened off with sliding doors for complete privacy. With its rough wooden shelving and old panelled cupboard, the space appears surprisingly humble given the priceless pieces of lacquerware, called *urushi*, created here.

IN THIS FARMHOUSE, the vast area under the roof has been converted into two levels of living space. This small sitting room is nestled under soot-blackened wooden beams bound with rice-straw rope. The steep pitch of the roof is typical of houses from Japan's snow country.

A DISTINCTIVE FEATURE of many farmhouses is the huge, rough-hewn ceiling beams that span the entire width of each structure. The pine wood throughout the houses has been blackened by centuries of wood smoke from the open hearths, which were common in country homes.

IN THE *GENKAN*, a custom-built storage cupboard with sliding doors blends in seamlessly with the aged farmhouse timbers. Shoes and house slippers are kept inside, enabling a smooth transition from outside to inside. For stepping out into the garden, a wooden pair of *geta* sit ready.

THE *ZASHIKI,* or reception room, overlooks a landscaped garden – a place for viewing rather than working or sitting in. *Sudare,* or reed blinds, hang the length of the *engawa,* or veranda, and can be unfurled in summer to give shade from the sun

ONE OF THE SMALLEST tea rooms at Mushakoji Senke, and the most informal, the *Gyoshutei* (Gliding Boat Hall) is so called because the ceiling resembles the hull of a boat. The ceiling and the raised window overlooking the garden are meant to evoke a summer boat trip on the river.

THE *SHOJI* SCREENS of this tea room slide back to reveal the garden, providing a meditative view for the guests of the tea ceremony. The entire scene captures the sense of calm simplicity which is crucial to the tea ceremony, offering an escape from the troubled outside world.

WITH GLASS WALLS that make the bathroom seem surrounded by trees, this room is a superb example of how this house has been designed to bring inside and outside together. The bathroom is understandably the owner's favourite place to unwind and relax after working all week in Tokyo.

A VARIETY OF Japanese bathrooms. With baths of wood, stone, or more modern materials; and heated by natural springs, or wood-fired burners, they each provide the most tranquil of environments for bathing.

THIS BATHROOM epitomises a clever mix of ages-old
Japanese aesthetics and modern practicality. Modelled on
the traditional Japanese *o-furo*, yet with the advantage of
modern plumbing, the bathroom resembles a miniature
bathhouse, with a tiled, drained floor – where the bather
perches on a wooden stool to soap up, wash and rinse –
and a cypress tub for soaking.

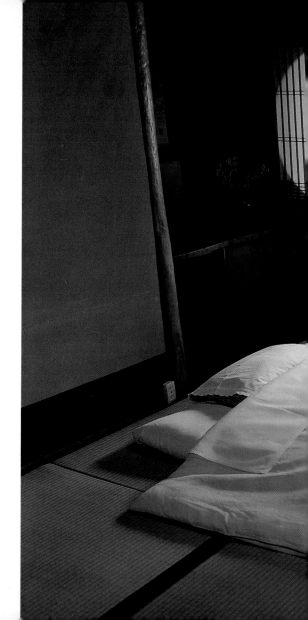

AS EVENING FALLS, staff at a *ryokan* pull futons and bedding from cupboards concealed behind sliding *fusuma* doors. A guest returns from a day out to find the low table and seats removed to one side and a futon laid out in their place. A thick *kaki-buton*, or quilt, on top of the futon provides warmth. An antique lacquered *andon*, or floor lamp, is set alongside; as is a carefully folded cotton kimono, called a *yukata*, and waist tie.

WHAT APPEARS TO BE a simple tatami room is in fact designed to project an air of refinement befitting an Imperial villa. The tatami mats are edged with an elegant brocade, while the *tokonoma* alcove is in the formal *shoin* style of the nobility, with an unusual circular *shoji* window.

149

A TATAMI ROOM in the late eighteenth-century farmhouse serves as a guest room. Low folding screens were traditionally arranged next to the futon to shield the guest from draughts. This particular screen depicts a hedge of chrysanthemums and dates fom the eighteenth century.

ALTHOUGH FURNISHED with a Western-style bed, the mood of
this bedroom is overwhelmingly Japanese. At the end of the
bed sits a low table for calligraphy, set with inks and antique
writing utensils, and a brush stand.

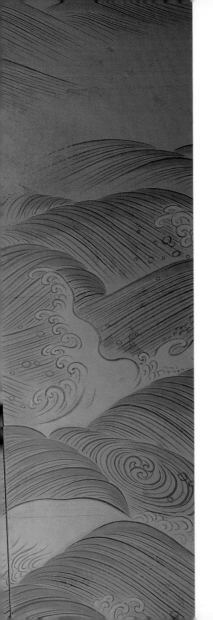

RARE ANTIQUE SCREENS depicting natural scenes.

AS WAS TYPICAL of kitchens in substantial Japanese houses built prior to the
twentieth century, the massive stove was wood-fired and compriseda series of
built-in cooking pots, each a different size and fitted with a wooden lid.
Around the stove, parts of the original earthenware floor are still visible.

THE CEDAR WALLS of the dining area are coloured ebony from two centuries of smoke from the cooking hearth (now replaced by a wood-burning stove); and a gold-toned cypress *mizuya dansu*, or kitchen dresser, provides ample household storage space.

161

LIKE THE SUBTLE gradations of tone found in the indigo-dyed fabrics, hanging here waiting to be treated, the wood surfaces in the house reveal an equally varied patina. Red-toned cedar doors in the living room slide back to reveal a stepped chest of drawers, called a *kaidan dansu* (which leads to a sleeping loft).

AN IMPRESSIVE LACQUERED elm *mizuya dansu*, or kitchen dresser, dominates one wall of a tatami guest room. This was once the tea room into which nobles were welcomed through a special entrance. The *dansu* holds a diverse collection of porcelain, including antique blue and white Imari ware and bolder contemporary pieces by local potter Kami Miki.

Architectural Elements

TATAMI   More than any other component of the Japanese house, tatami is the core around which almost all residential architecture revolves. In essence a floor covering woven from straw, the rectangular tatami mat is found in almost every house in the country. Even modern homes will include one tatami room; essentially a tea room, but also a guest room where futons can be unfurled at night. The origin of tatami stretches back to ancient Japanese civilisation, when straw was spread over a bare earth floor to provide softness and warmth.

BAMBOO   Historical texts reveal that in Japan bamboo once had over 1400 practical and decorative uses. In the Japanese house, bamboo is a common and expected feature. A bamboo fence is often the first point of contact between the street and the rest of the house. Bamboo is also the favoured material for the ceilings and rafters of traditional farmhouses and country dwellings. Bamboo, or sometimes reed, is used to fashion the external blinds, called *sudare*, that shield the façade of a house from the intense heat of the sun, and which replace *shoji* doors in summer to aid ventilation.

PAPER   Novelist Junichiro Tanizaki wrote that 'the beauty of a Japanese room depends on a variation of shadows, heavy shadows against light shadows'. This mystery of shadows is in fact engineered by the expert use of paper as a building and decorative material. It is handmade paper, or *washi*, that gives the Japanese house its moody and atmospheric interior. There are hundreds of handmade papers each suited to a particular purpose depending on its character.

WOOD   Perhaps the most precious and revered of all materials, wood has until the late twentieth century been the most accessible of materials, cut from the forests that cover Japan's mountainous interior. Pine, cedar and cypress trees have all grown in abundance, although these woods are now increasingly viewed as a finite, restricted and expensive resource. Nevertheless, most house construction is still based on a timber framework as it has been for centuries, and the carpenter is the most respected of artisans. Wood, however, is much more than simply a building material. In interiors, its warmth, its irregularities and texture are considered important aesthetic elements.

STONE   Stone, like timber, is valued for its individuality. Single large rocks can form the centrepiece of a Japanese garden – the peculiar colouring, texture and shape of each one contributing significantly to the mood of the landscaping. Flat, irregular-shaped pieces of stone are used for footpaths and to pave entranceways. When scrubbed or hosed with water – shining in the early morning sun, or glowing in the light of a lantern – stone can take on poetic qualities.

168